Handwriting: Cursive

Grades 3-5

CARSON-DELLOSA®
PUBLISHING GROUP

Greensboro, NC 27425 USA

Brighter Child®
An imprint of Carson-Dellosa Publishing LLC
P.O. Box 35665
Greensboro, NC 27425 USA

Printed in the U.S.A. • All rights reserved.

ISBN 978-1-4838-1643-2

08-071187784

Aa

Practice by tracing the letter. Then, write the letter.

a a a a a

a a a a a

Bb

Practice by tracing the letter. Then, write the letter.

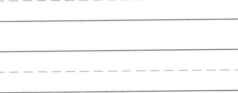

Cc

Practice by tracing the letter. Then, write the letter.

C C C C C

C C C C C

Dd

Practice by tracing the letter. Then, write the letter.

$\mathcal{D}$ $\mathcal{D}$ $\mathcal{D}$ $\mathcal{D}$ $\mathcal{D}$

d d d d d

Ee

Practice by tracing the letter. Then, write the letter.

Ff

Practice by tracing the letter. Then, write the letter.

Gg

Practice by tracing the letter. Then, write the letter.

Hh

Practice by tracing the letter. Then, write the letter.

H H H H H H

h h h h h h

Ii

Practice by tracing the letter. Then, write the letter.

Jj

Practice by tracing the letter. Then, write the letter.

Kk

Practice by tracing the letter. Then, write the letter.

K K K K K K

k k k k k k

Ll

Practice by tracing the letter. Then, write the letter.

$\mathcal{L}$ $\mathcal{L}$ $\mathcal{L}$ $\mathcal{L}$ $\mathcal{L}$ $\mathcal{L}$

ℓ ℓ ℓ ℓ ℓ ℓ

Mm

Practice by tracing the letter. Then, write the letter.

m m m m m

m m m m m

Nn

Practice by tracing the letter. Then, write the letter.

_n n n n n_

_m m m m m_

Oo

Practice by tracing the letter. Then, write the letter.

17 *Handwriting: Cursive*

Pp

Practice by tracing the letter. Then, write the letter.

$\mathcal{P}$ $\mathcal{P}$ $\mathcal{P}$ $\mathcal{P}$ $\mathcal{P}$ $\mathcal{P}$ $\mathcal{P}$

$\mathcal{p}$ $\mathcal{p}$ $\mathcal{p}$ $\mathcal{p}$ $\mathcal{p}$ $\mathcal{p}$

Qq

Practice by tracing the letter. Then, write the letter.

Rr

Practice by tracing the letter. Then, write the letter.

Ss

Practice by tracing the letter. Then, write the letter.

Tt

Practice by tracing the letter. Then, write the letter.

Uu

Practice by tracing the letter. Then, write the letter.

U U U U U U

UU UU UU UU UU

Vv

Practice by tracing the letter. Then, write the letter.

Ww

Practice by tracing the letter. Then, write the letter.

$\mathcal{W}$ $\mathcal{W}$ $\mathcal{W}$ $\mathcal{W}$ $\mathcal{W}$

w w w w w

Xx

Practice by tracing the letter. Then, write the letter.

Yy

Practice by tracing the letter. Then, write the letter.

Yy Yy Yy Yy Yy

ny y y y y

Zz

Practice by tracing the letter. Then, write the letter.

Aa Words

Practice by tracing the words. Then, write the words.

an

and

animals

April

Bb Words

Practice by tracing the words. Then, write the words.

big

boy

babble

baboon

Cc Words

Practice by tracing the words. Then, write the words.

can

candy

cool

count

Dd Words

Practice by tracing the words. Then, write the words.

do

dog

dandelions

donuts

Name _____

Ee Words

Practice by tracing the words. Then, write the words.

© Carson-Dellosa

33

Handwriting: Cursive

Ff Words

Practice by tracing the words. Then, write the words.

far

fat

fluff

feast

Gg Words

Practice by tracing the words. Then, write the words.

good

Handwriting: Cursive

Hh Words

Practice by tracing the words. Then, write the words.

his

happy

he

hello

Ii Words

Practice by tracing the words. Then, write the words.

if

in

idea

itch

Jj Words

Practice by tracing the words. Then, write the words.

jam

job

jazz

junk

Kk Words

Practice by tracing the words. Then, write the words.

kid

key

Kick

keep

Ll Words

Practice by tracing the words. Then, write the words.

low

land

lamb

little

Mm Words

Practice by tracing the words. Then, write the words.

mad

milk

monkeys

merry

41 *Handwriting: Cursive*

Nn Words

Practice by tracing the words. Then, write the words.

nap

name

near

night

42

Oo Words

Practice by tracing the words. Then, write the words.

out

often

once

order

Handwriting: Cursive

Pp Words

Practice by tracing the words. Then, write the words.

pan

pet

pick

paper

Qq Words

Practice by tracing the words. Then, write the words.

quit

quick

quart

quiet

Rr Words

Practice by tracing the words. Then, write the words.

rat

run

rear

road

Ss Words

Practice by tracing the words. Then, write the words.

see

sing

stand

stow

Tt Words

Practice by tracing the words. Then, write the words.

the

tip

told

twist

Uu Words

Practice by tracing the words. Then, write the words.

use

under

until

unhappy

Vv Words

Practice by tracing the words. Then, write the words.

vest

Ww Words

Practice by tracing the words. Then, write the words.

wet

west

wall

winter

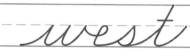

51 *Handwriting: Cursive*

Xx Words

Practice by tracing the words. Then, write the words.

x-ray

box

extra

xylophone

X-RAY
MACHINE

FOX IN BOX

Yy Words

Practice by tracing the words. Then, write the words.

you

yard

year

yellow

Zz Words

Practice by tracing the words. Then, write the words.

zero

zoom

zone

zipper

Write Sentences

Write the sentence.

Arctic animals act amusingly.

Write Sentences

Write the sentence.

Big baboons

break balloons.

Write Sentences

Write the sentence.

Cool crocodiles

count coconuts.

Write Sentences

Write the sentence.

Dogs deliver dandelions and donuts.

Write Sentences

Write the sentence.

Electric eels eat excitedly.

59

Write Sentences

Write the sentence.

Flamingos fluff fancy feathers.

Write Sentences

Write the sentence.

Giggling gophers give gag gifts.

Write Sentences

Write the sentence.

Happy hippos hang in their hammocks.

Write Sentences

Write the sentence.

Insects itch in the infield.

Handwriting: Cursive

Write Sentences

Write the sentence.

Juggling jaguars jam to jazz.

Write Sentences

Write the sentence.

Kooky kangaroos

kick in karate.

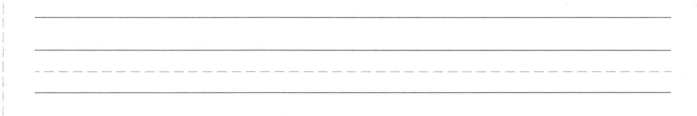

Write Sentences

Write the sentence.

Little lambs lick lemon lollipops.

Write Sentences

Write the sentence.

Merry monkeys make marmalade.

Write Sentences

Write the sentence.

Naughty gnats never nap at night.

Write Sentences

Write the sentence.

Ostriches often order onion omelettes.

Write Sentences

Write the sentence.

Pandas paint pictures on paper.

Write Sentences

Write the sentence.

Quick quails quarrel over a unique quarter.

Write Sentences

Write the sentence.

Raccoons run races in red cars.

Write Sentences

Write the sentence.

Standing storks

sing with swans.

Write Sentences

Write the sentence.

Two tigers tickle the other's toes.

Write Sentences

Write the sentence.

Unicorns use umbrellas under thunder.

Write Sentences

Write the sentence.

Vultures vacuum in velvet vests.

Write Sentences

Write the sentence.

Wet walruses

bowl to win.

Write Sentences

Write the sentence.

Xandra x-rays boxes with foxes.

Write Sentences

Write the sentence.

Yaks yell and yodel loudly.

79

Handwriting: Cursive

Write Sentences

Write the sentence.

Zigzagging zebras zip and zoom.